The Wig-Maker

ALSO BY SHARON THESEN

Artemis Hates Romance
Radio New France Radio
Holding the Pose
Confabulations
The Beginning of the Long Dash
The Pangs of Sunday: Selected Poems
Aurora
News and Smoke: Selected Poems
A Pair of Scissors
Weeping Willow
The Good Bacteria
Oyama Pink Shale
The Receiver

For Ross and Joan,

with much love

The Wig-Maker

JANET GALLANT

SHARON THESEN

VANCOUVER

NEW STAR BOOKS

2021

 NEW STAR BOOKS LTD
#107–3477 Commercial St, Vancouver, BC V5N 4E8 CANADA
1574 Gulf Road, #1517 Point Roberts, WA 98281 USA
newstarbooks.com ·
info@newstarbooks.com

The publisher acknowledges the financial support of the Canada Council for the Arts, the British Columbia Arts Council, and the Government of Canada.

Cataloguing information for this book is available from Library and Archives Canada, www.collectionscanada.gc.ca.

Cover design by Oliver McPartlin
Typeset by New Star Books
Printed and bound in Canada by Imprimerie Gauvin, Gatineau, QC

First printing March 2021

To Samantha and Nicole
my reason, my heart.
May you forever find peace and joy in the flight of the hummingbird.

Remembering is not a passionate or dispassionate retelling of a reality that is no more, but a new birth of the past, when time goes in reverse. Above all, it is creativity. As they narrate, people create, they "write" their life ... They draw the words out of themselves, not from newspapers and books they have read, not from others.

Svetlana Alexievich, *The Unwomanly Face of War: An Oral History of Women in World War II*

introduction
Janet Gallant

My name is Janet, and I am a wig-maker. I haven't always been a wig-maker. For over twenty-five years I was an executive assistant for various businesses in Calgary. At the age of forty-five I was diagnosed with alopecia, by forty-six I was bald. There on the floor and clogged in the shower drain was my thick curly hair. After a couple of frustrating years and a several thousand dollars spent on off-the-rack wigs, I wasn't satisfied. The fit was never quite right, the hairline didn't look natural. I didn't feel like me. So, my journey into the craft of wig-making began.

I found a $100 course online that taught me the basics. I learned how to create a custom foundation; made of fine film-grade lace, sections stitched together, darts formed and secured using invisible thread and a ventilating tool (a small barbed hook). Human hairs are pulled through the lace holes with the tiny hook, knotted two hairs, three hairs, sometimes one hair at a time. Thousands of hours would be spent pulling hairs at the kitchen table. The best wig-makers can pull fast, and achieve knots that are so tight, the average eye mistakes them for the real thing.

After practicing at the kitchen table for about year, I was hired by an established wig-maker to work on a few projects. This opportunity provided me with valuable tricks of the trade and helped me take my wig making skills to the next level. After another year of practice and literally thousands and thousands of hair strands later, my wig making business was born.

I was born in, and for the most part, raised in Calgary. My father was in the army. His postings took us from CFB Calgary (Sarcee PMQs), to CFB Gagetown (Oromocto, NB) to CFB Downsview (Toronto), and finally back to Calgary (Currie PMQs) by the time I was eleven years old. I currently live with my partner Jim in Lake Country, BC, on a woodland treed lot, situated on a quiet cul-de-sac on the side of a mountain overlooking Lake Okanagan.

Our view of the lake is from the upper-level deck off the master bedroom. A tiny sliver of a lake view is all we have, due to the row of houses between our home and the lake. One of the houses blocking our view is where our neighbours Sharon and Paul live. They were our first friends when we moved into the neighbourhood in December of 2014.

Paul and my Jim are avid cyclists (mountains, roads, sun or snow) and it didn't take long for them to become riding buddies. Sharon and I had a friendly relationship for the first couple years, hellos as we came and went on the cul-de-sac. Friendly waves while shovelling in winter, while picking up the pine needles in spring.

I would often start my day with a smile as I'd watch Sharon and their dog Boomer, a standard poodle with a curly apricot coat, collect the morning newspaper. I'd watch them perform their daily ritual from the deck off our master bedroom. Out of the front door would come Sharon, wrapped tight in her house coat, pj's peeking out the bottom, in her slippers. Boomer would bound around the front yard garden, sometimes distracted by a chipmunk, or maybe the quail moving through, Sharon would have to call him a time or two. He would come, happily, like clockwork he'd take the newspaper from Sharon's hand, that was his job. Into the house they would go, time for coffee and the news. A sweet way to start my day, watching Sharon and Boomer.

On July 15, 2017, I was alone in the house with our bichon shih tzu Mindy, working on a wig project for a wig-maker that caters to the film and TV industry. It was "fire season". The annual summer dry season has meant forest fires here in the interior of BC. There had been fire stories in the news again that week, but focussing on my deadline, I was unaware of the fire raging just a couple of kilometres away. Paul knew Jim was away visiting his father in Drumheller and had business appointments in Calgary, so he was checking up on me, making sure I was not alone. From Paul I learned about this new fire that was threatening our neighbourhood.

A few of us gathered at Sharon and Paul's place to wait it out together. To see if the winds would work for, or against us this hot summer evening. Waiting to hear if we would have to evacuate.

As we nibbled on snacks and sipped on wine, as the airtankers buzzed the sky, Sharon and I began the conversation that is this story. The conversation that gave me the courage to tell. Somewhere between the chips and salsa, and my second glass of red, our friendship began. I remember how easy it was to talk with Sharon. There was no small talk. I can't explain it, my heart trusted her heart. By evenings end the winds would blow in our favour. Sadly, eight homes were lost to the fire, luckily there were no casualties.

Several days later, this time without wine, we sat together again, and it was decided. Sharon offered to take the pen, somehow she knew I was ready to tell, needed to tell. At first, we'd meet once a month, then every couple of weeks, later, thanks to publishing deadlines, every few days. I'd talk, Sharon would listen, and type. I'd cry, Sharon would cry with me, and type. Many times, I would be struggling to express myself, I'd be without words to articulate certain feelings. But these are the moments that would keep us both going. In these moments, Sharon would pull one of her books from the overstuffed, floor-to-ceiling bookshelves. Without hesitation, she would flip through a few pages, scrolling swiftly over the words with her finger, then she would recite a passage or two. Each time presenting parallels that would go above and beyond analogy. It really was, and continues to be, magical, this collaboration, this friendship.

We are writing this book, due to my lifelong need to tell the story of my brother Billy, dead by suicide before his fourteenth birthday; to tell the story of our sister Penny, dead at the age of forty, ravaged by breast cancer after suffering, her entire adult life, on the streets of Canada with schizophrenia. The story of innocence lost, taken by the one called father, overlooked by the lady of the house. A story of three generations of women (my grandmother, my mother, and my sister Penny) whose lives, and loved ones, were taken by the same mental illness.

My friend Melissa asked me if music would be woven into this telling. She knows how important music was to me, is to me. I told her I hadn't considered it at that point. She got me thinking. I look forward to following up with Melissa, to let her know how it worked out. To let her know the music is indeed here. Lyrics of truth, and notes of healing, are here.

I would tell Melissa that an editor friend of mine, an admirer of Sharon's poetic talents, helped me answer this one. He was kind enough to provide me with guidance as I wrote this introduction. I quote him below. I think he answers Melissa's question, beautifully.

"Most of us think of poetry as having come out of music, or at least out of the same place that music comes. A term used to describe Sharon is that she is a 'lyric poet,' poetry being the lyrics to invisible songs.

You and Sharon are singing together."

questions unanswered

Now I understand where the names come from
    I know which slave owner owned us
        but I didn't know my mother

I didn't even know my mother was Black
I was ten or eleven
    Dad said, one time when I made a mean comment
        well, your mother's Black.
From then on, every time I saw a Black woman
    I would watch her.

I always wanted to be a singer
    always idolized Diana Ross
        and began to daydream my mom looked like Diana Ross

I was about three when my mom left.

Abandoning your children
   where does that come from?
      So much loss in the early days, diphtheria, the Trail of Tears

I looked at the census documents on the Ellis Norman farm in Texas
   They didn't even write their names down
      Just numbers and what they were worth
It sickens me that the African names were lost
   Part of the grief I've had is all that was stolen from us
      Stories, language, forgiveness, remembering, ceremony

African-Americans in the late 1800s—
   The records the Normans and Johnsons kept were just the
                                names of the slave owners.
   My mother's name, Valerie "Johnson."

Why can't I find any history on those families?
   They're lying about it still,
      Still riding the backs of Black people in Texas.
And the backs of Mexicans, too.

I didn't learn about this until I saw *Roots*.
   I learned about the pyramids, industrialization, the Ford people.
      If you grew up like me you didn't know.

My mom ran away from it all.
   My whole life I've had this yearning
      but loss just comes

No aunts or uncles ever looked for us. Not one
   of the matriarchs of the family in each generation
      changed or healed, not one of them fessed up

Not one of them had the courage or the strength to make the change.
   How easy it was for them to just leave us.
      It was the wrong choice where the children were concerned.

You can't be a mentally ill woman at home with four children.
   You can't be alone; servicemen would be away for months at
                                                        a time.
      There was no community support.

Dad was called home because the children were not being properly
                                                     taken care of.
It all fell apart, my mom left.

Then Doreen arrived. Doreen was Black, too.

She moved in with her little daughter a year younger than me.
After that my dad got posted to CFB Downsview and
Doreen came with us.

There she was on the census: Doreen "housekeeper," Doreen "cook."
You can't have a Black woman you're not married to
answering the door.
Not on an army base.

Dad never divorced my mom, I don't think he'd even married
my mom.
He never married Doreen, never signed anything.
It wasn't a loving partnership.

There we were on the army base surrounded by white homemakers
all looking down on us, these kids, all different colors.

I saw myself as a white girl.
My dad was white, blue-green eyes.
I would say to Doreen, *you will never be my mother.*

I was prejudiced when I was a child
and didn't understand what it meant.
My dad hated fat people, he was homophobic.

He'd make fun of my sister, she had a problem with her left foot

and knee
and call her a fuckin' ox —
who can call their child an ox?

But at least he didn't leave us.
We can say that. But only because
he didn't want to look like a loser on the outside.

You reap what you sow.

He rotted away from diabetes, smoked two packs a day until he
died age 69.
He threw all his family pictures away.
Aunt Elizabeth said she found them all in the garbage.
He died really lonely.

You reap what you sow.

to go to 2002, windsor

At times I thought my father had killed my mother.
It was my stepsister who found my mother was living in Windsor.
    It was 2002. My stepsister had been looking
        for her own bio-dad and took it upon herself
           to snoop for my mom and she found her.
And I am grateful.

Windsor: dirty, ominous, burning, like when Dad burned the chair
    falling asleep drunk, smoking.
        I was already prepared for this.

My mom ran away from it all.
    I was around three. She was a shadowy presence at the top of
                  the stairs.
        We never saw her again. No pictures, no birthday cards,
                 no phone calls.

Then, when I went to Windsor —
    a three hundred and fifty pound vegetable, very mentally ill,
    didn't seem to even want to know me.

Her husband at the time, I got the impression he was living off
    the mental illness benefits my mom received from the
                government.

My sister Penny was dying of cancer at this time.
    There was nothing I could bring back to her.
        Except pity.

My mother's first-born son was taken away from her.
    She was told he was stillborn.
Her second-born was Penny.
        Penny's father was most likely my mom's previous employer.
            Then, with my dad, she had Billy, then me, then Ian.

Mentally ill post-partum hormones ripping.
    Then Beverley about six years later, after she'd left us.
        I wouldn't be surprised if she'd cranked out more kids in
                                 between.

I want to find my eldest brother.

Auntie Crystal and Aunt Judy
said *they know for a fact*
that boy was not stillborn
and did not die later.

Auntie Crystal saw him *with her own eyes*
in Edmonton
and someone said, *Oh, there's Cory, Valerie's boy!*

The family must have known
and certainly Valerie's stepmother knew
even then that my mom wasn't capable
was mentally ill
was probably raped.

In those days, in Wildwood, Alberta
who would know?

In Wildwood at that time there would be no adoption records.
They must have thought they were doing the right thing.

tom

My dad didn't say a lot
    but he had only wonderful things to say about his grandmother
        his mother and his sister. He never talked about his father.
I never knew anything else about anyone else in his family.
    His sister-in-law told me
        And this was before I told her about the abuse,
"Our priest was not part of that. I will tell you, though,
    Your grandfather was nicknamed 'the pervert.'
        Your grandmother wouldn't let the children out of her sight."

I would love to talk to Aunt Elizabeth!
    "Can you tell me if my dad went to church? Aunt Elizabeth,
        aren't you wondering why your Tommy died with no family by his side?"
My father may as well have hung himself.
But she's ignoring me. Her entire family has shut down,
    won't contact me. His brothers—Uncle Walter, a bus driver—
        I've met once. He's in denial, a nice enough guy, nothing to say.
Uncle Bud never called me either. He's dead now.

I think it's really important to know
    why my dad was such a monster.
        Was it the military — or was it his own father — or was
            it the Church?
        Aunt Elizabeth said to me, "our priest was not part
            of that."
At 22 he's got Penny, Billy, and me.
    He only had a Grade Eight or Nine education.
        How poor he was as a kid in Halifax, Nova Scotia.

Raising five kids on a soldier's salary
    must have been incredibly hard.
        My dad could have given us away but he didn't.
What if I had been separated from all my siblings, adopted out or
            fostered?

He must have been lonely after my mom left.
  He never had a love in his life after her.
    He didn't love Doreen, he ignored her.
The only reason she came into our lives was as a housekeeper,
  a caregiver for us kids.
    Once he played the guitar and sang to us, trying to be a dad.
      "Jimmy crack corn and I don't care
      The master's gone away."
He taught himself to play the guitar while he was in Egypt and Cyprus.

I didn't realize about the sexual abuse until I was older.

to begin with

No one knows what happened to my mom's first-born son.
Of the four kids she had while living with my dad, two have died —
    Penny became a homeless addict, prostitute, and mental patient.
        She died of breast cancer at the age of forty.
            Billy's death was horrendous, a suicide at age
                            fourteen after a lifetime
of physical and emotional abuse by our father.

Dad sexually abused me, Penny, and our stepsister.

It began for me in kindergarten.
He was already raping Penny by that time.
By the time I was in Grade Nine
my dad was calling me for "tea-time" — "Janet,
come down and bring me some tea," he would say
from the basement. Doreen would be crocheting or watching TV.
I would take the tea downstairs and my father would
open his fly.

I'd go back upstairs and brush my teeth.

With Penny, he had intercourse. With me and my stepsister,
he didn't.

I thought my dad favoured me by not wanting to get me pregnant.

the neighbour

The next-door neighbour, red-headed Irish or Scottish.
I'll never forget him.
    I was in kindergarten and went over to play with his son.
        It was time to go home so he sent his son to bed
And took me down to the basement.
    Just like tea-time with my dad.
        Somehow he knew I wouldn't tell, and I didn't.

I'm in Toronto in Grade Two, Grade Three, Grade Four
    looking for boys' attention, older big boys
        who wanted to touch me. That's what love meant.

My dad was such a liar.
    It was all about perception, I had to be a refined lady
        I never carried myself like a slut, not even nail polish.
I was perfect.
    I fooled them all, to the point where I fooled myself.
        I was fictitious. I wore nice suits.

By the time you're six, you're a double agent.

In a world that feels this way, the soul knows something is wrong.
The moan is the vibrations of the soul.

Since I could never speak my truths, how could I sing them?
I never felt worthy. I felt like a fraud.

The truth is in music. The truth is in the moan. Billy's moan.
The moan on the slave ships.

Everything that is wrong is in this story.

In one of the few existing photos from Janet's childhood, you see a piece of half-dead scrappy lawn and a shabby building wall; her father sitting & smoking on a set of plain wooden steps leading to a front door. Doreen's brother sits beside him.

Janet talks about stairs, tops of stairs, bottoms of stairs where the door opened onto, and where Tom nearly killed Penny when he came charging through the door one time raging drunk.

It was at the top of the stairs that Janet's mother stood, a shadowy presence now in memory, but at the time, the last glimpse of her mother three-year-old Janet had.

There were likely no goodbyes, at least no meaningful or memorable ones. It's possible her mother went out to meet some friends that night and never returned. Tom later told Janet her mother had run off with another man, her mother was a whore. How he'd caught her before that, saying she was going out to meet a girlfriend but had "fancy clothes" stuffed in her handbag.

Janet remembers an *energy of fear* around this time.

As for downstairs, that is where Tom fooled around with screws and bolts pretending to make things, and where Janet would later undergo tea time. She remembers hearing the "ting" sound of small metal things being dropped into containers. Soon would come his request for a cup of tea.

best friend tracy

Tracy was my bestie from junior high.
    Her father Carl was in the military police.
        He was strict but lovely, playful—called her "Peanut."

I envied their loving playful goofy —
    He enjoyed having his daughter. Her mother
    kept the house immaculate.
Tracy got pregnant by a Black man
    and her mother disowned her.
        Tracy has been estranged from her mom & her dad for
                thirty years.
All because mommy Sheila doesn't like the way her
            grandchildren look.

Tracy is the most loving, beautiful mother.
    She adopted a couple of kids.
        She has twenty-two grandchildren and she's fifty-one
             years old.
She knows more about love than they do.
    Carl is still hanging onto "Peanut."
        He won't be with her, he won't support her.
Because he's got to be with his wife.

I'll never forget: Tracy and I had electric shavers for our legs,
    her mom underneath us vacuuming.

penny

(Penny Susan Johnson was born in 1963 and her death in 2003 was the outcome of a lifetime of suffering and living on the streets for half of her life.

Symptoms of mental illness appeared shortly after Billy committed suicide.)

Penny was always different.
    The mental illness was in her blood.
By the age of seventeen she had so much tragedy
    she didn't have a chance of ever being a well-functioning
                                   mental patient
        living an almost-normal life. But add drugs
and alcohol and
    finding dear Billy hanging in the closet.

She was already a fragile young lady
    she never hurt anyone except herself.
        Immediately after finding Billy dead she got pregnant.
She was too far gone to have an abortion
        estranged from her family the last four months of her
                                   pregnancy.
        She was sent to the Louise Dean School for
                        Unwed Mothers
so she could finish high school and have her baby taken from her.
        Young Michael is born in March 1981.
        He was given up for adoption.

Penny was diagnosed with schizophrenia.
She always wished Michael had a good life,
a better life than hers.
Penny was pregnant again soon,
went on to have another son, James.
Promiscuity is part of an abused woman's life.
She never received any therapy for anything.
Nobody talked, nobody hugged, it wasn't part of our upbringing.

My father the monster decides James is not going to be adopted.

He and Doreen took James away from her
but it was probably the best thing for James at the time,
though Doreen would leave my dad soon after that.
They had a "shared custody" arrangement.

Penny started disappearing for three or four years at a time.
Jails, hospitals, drugs, prostitution.
Ten years went by before I ever saw her again.

I called her doctor: "she needs to be committed, she's living on
the streets."
The doctor said to me,
young lady, she has schizophrenia move on with your life
and hung up.

All Penny ever wanted was for her boys to be together.

All she ever worried about was her sons.

All she ever wanted was to be normal.

While I'm making wigs I'm watching a TV show called *Long Lost Family*.

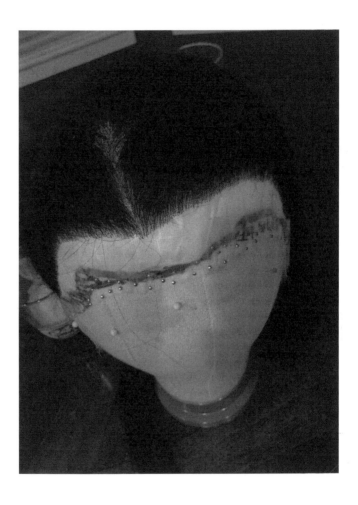

Janet has begun a home business making wigs. When she is making a wig, Janet is "ventilating," threading hairs one, two, three at a time into a lace foundation, the lace so fine as to be almost invisible, a veil of pierced shimmer carefully placed onto the naked straw-filled canvas-skinned "block head". Using a heavy mounted magnifying glass, she works from the nape past the occiput and up around the crown, threading hairs in here and there at random. since each wig is an original and must look natural. Eventually there comes a moment when she feels there is someone in the room with her—a life, a fate, a personality. At that point, Janet starts referring to a person in progress, a "she."

Each piece starts with the foundation.
  A lace form mimicking every curve, nape to forehead, ear to ear.
   SHE shows up as the profile work begins,
    the emergence of the hairline.
Almost alive now.

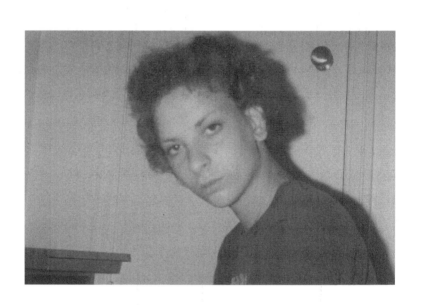

penny

She was thirty-eight, I was thirty-five the first time either of us
spoke about the sexual abuse
  in detail. We talked about a lot of stuff.
    Our mother left us when she was seven, I was around three.
Penny was old enough to watch her mother walk out of the door.
    The sexual abuse started with her before it started with me.
      Doreen knew. I wonder if Valerie knew.
The schizophrenia just let Penny be mad at the world.

She died peacefully on a winter morning, December 30, 2003.
    I was relieved. We'd said everything we had to say.
      And I'm talking *everything*.

Penny was never checked by doctors as a baby.
    She was pigeon-toed and never given braces or therapies.
      Tom would make fun of her, call her an ox.
But she still managed to flutter her way through life.

I'm in Grade Six, she's in junior high, with all those things against her,
    an awkward-looking girl, a girl that's bullied and teased
      but she's on the cheerleading squad, cute as a button,
costumes, pom-poms, running down the stairs

She was able to be cheerful and funny.

All that was gone the day my brother died.

the visit

I'm thirty-five years old.
    Penny is thirty-nine, living the last year of her life
        with me, in Calgary.
The phone rings, it's my stepsister, she says "I know where your mom is."

The next thing I know I'm flying to Windsor to meet my mom.
    I haven't seen or heard from her in over thirty years.
        No calls, no presents, no cards, nothing.

Penny is way too sick to come with me.
    I'm twenty grand in debt taking care of her, I'm ninety-five pounds.
        I chose a hotel at the border crossing.

You can't sleep in a hotel anyway.
    Semis all night, brakes starting and stopping all night.
        Windsor stinks like old factories, abandoned industries.

My mom is living in a small apartment with her Jamaican husband.
    A three hundred and fifty pound vegetable propped in a chair.
        Sixty years old, diabetic, mentally ill.
            I never knew I was named after my mother's
                              middle name.

I spent my life pretending my mother was Diana Ross.
    My father told me she left with another man, my mom was a whore.
        All of that went away as soon as I saw her.

All the bad feelings went away.
She couldn't possibly have taken care of me.
She barely knew who I was.
I realized then and there Dad did the same things to her as he did to us.

She cranked out six kids in twelve years, mentally ill, hormones ripping.
She never had a chance to be a healthy mom. Her own mom
left, too.
And her grandmother was adopted. Three generations
of women

Abandoning their kids or being abandoned themselves.
I had nothing but pity and love and just wanted to hug her up.
I had nothing else.

I stayed in Windsor for two nights, had two three-hour visits with her.
There was no relationship to be had.
I could take that back to my sister.
She too could have peace.

My mom's been gone a long time. I don't even know if she's passed.
The latest response from Service Ontario is that there is no
record
Or registration of her death.

Men have to stop raping their children.
They never get over it.
It destroys lives.
It is always going to be with you.

I choose not to do the "woe is me" thing.

But a lot of people aren't strong enough.
Their lives are destroyed.
Like Penny.
Like my mom.
Even my horrible stepmom. Doreen died young.

She knew all about it.

Penny told me Doreen walked in on them.

We were taught not to tell anyone.
My sisters—we all thought we were the only one.

My stepsister from hell. She was horrible.
My dad was raping her too,
Now a hoarder, her children are a wreck too.
My father did that to her.

My dad hurt Doreen too.
I wish she could have been stronger.
She probably did the best she could.

Hating her can only kill me.

But I'm grateful I don't hate these people.
I would be this horrible awful drug addicted thing.
I'm sure I would be.

all the family photos

Doreen left Tom and her new husband was a gambler.
    They kept alienating landlords by not paying the rent on time.
    The last landlord they tried to rip off would not give
                                     them access
To their belongings
    Until they paid up.
        They never paid up.

Doreen kept all the family documents in a blue metal steamer chest
    that had all the pictures in it—photos, report cards,
        Billy's death certificate. The landlord got rid of it all.

In the late nineties both Doreen and my dad went back to the
Maritimes to die.
    She died in Oromocto; he died in Halifax.

Janet shows me one of the few photos she has of herself
as a child living at CFB Downsview. She's about ten at the
time, holding a League bowling trophy. Her friends Sally
and Susan's house is behind her. Thinking about it now,
she says, there was a guy living next door to Sally and
Susan's. He was at least eighteen, all up on her. Sticking
his tongue down her throat. She was nine or ten years old.
She was already just there for the taking, she says. It makes
her sick, she says. She never felt like a slum girl until she
saw this photo. Her father was away in Egypt almost a year
around that time, '77, '78. She never had any supervision,
would go to the park herself. "Just welfare kids," she says.

I think of Janet and her siblings living on army bases
in Alberta, Ontario, and New Brunswick. As kids in
school, we heard kids like them referred to as "army brats."
Amy brats didn't seem have roots or permanence in their
lives. What they had must have included familiarity with
parental absences, mutilating injuries, PTSD, militaristic
values. There was an aura of glamour around army brats;
they were close to the mysteries of faraway war zones,
to heroism, death, violence, politics, local and national
emergencies and disasters. The rest of us were careful
around their sacrificial power.

a whole new grief for penny

When I met with Michael's adoptive parents
    I realized a whole new grief for Penny.
        Little Michael was in foster care for fourteen days after he
                was born.
You can guess why.

His adoptive mom told me that the social worker called her
    to say "We have a baby, a boy
        but to be honest we've had some trouble placing him
Because of his African heritage."

I had to start seeing myself as a brown person
    although I didn't look like a brown person.
        A very powerful learning, that.

I had it easy, out of all my siblings.
    I was my dad's favourite. He spoke kindly to me
        when he wasn't abusing or yelling at me.

He tried to tell me I was special. My brothers were "useless twits."

Doreen called me "the sneaky one."
    "You're a sneaky little bitch aren't you."
        My role was to do the housework so no one would scream
        "You're a sneaky one aren't you!"

Going to school in New Brunswick, kindergarten and Grade One.
　　It was wonderful for me because it was outside the family.
　　　　I was so good at school. Me and this boy Richie.

Our teacher would have a contest—who could do cursive homework
　　And Richie and I would compete.
　　　　He would win, or I would.

He had beautiful penmanship and was always nice to me.
　　The most precious times were getting pats on the back
　　　　from my teacher for my handwriting.

No one ever hugged us.

The day of Billy's funeral was the only time
　　Doreen held me like a mother
　　　　is supposed to hold a child.
We were all sitting in a pew together.
　　My dad reaches his hand over.
　　　　I thought he was grabbing my hand
But he was only asking for a tissue.

billy

We live on 20th St. in CFB Calgary, just south of my favorite ice
cream shop.
It's July, a beautiful sunny gorgeous July day.
Billy is grounded again, probably for smoking.
Or my dad just got pissed off and grounded him.

Billy's bedroom is across the hall from the linen closet
I'm heading up there to grab some towels
Going swimming with my friend Liz and my stepsister.
Billy's lying on his bottom bunkbed.
He shared a room with Ian.
He's lying on his bed playing with a bicycle lock
Chain, spin, dials, coloured plastic.
He says, "Do you want to play cards?"
And I say "as soon as I come home.
It's so nice out why don't you get outside, get some fresh air?
Ask Dad if you can walk the dog."
He says,
"I'm not asking that fucking asshole anything I'm not asking nothing.
He doesn't give a fuck about me."
"Okay," I say, "when I get home we'll hang out."

Me and Liz go to the army barracks where the swimming pool was.
Two, three hours later we get home and Ian, nine years old, is outside
bouncing the basketball on the sidewalk.
Looks at me and says, "Dad wants to talk to you."
The number one rule is you take your swimsuit and towel and
hang it up to dry.
I go to the back yard to do so. When I entered the house
Dad is sitting at the bottom of the stairs, which is strange.
I kind of look in the house and there's two Catholic collars and
my stepmom Doreen.
"Did your brother say anything to you before you left?"
"No, why?"
"Janet your brother is dead. He hung himself in the closet with
the bicycle lock."
It was the first time he ever hugged me.
"Penny found him."

That night I went to bed. What if what if what if. What if.

I was eleven years old and Billy was the most wonderful boy.
    So what if he smoked a cigarette? He never hurt anyone.
    He was my friend, the kind you played cards with.

Dad had sent Penny upstairs to get Billy out to mow the lawn.
    Penny was fifteen and a half.
        By the time she was seventeen she was giving birth to
                                                            Michael.

That night I go to bed. It's a dream it's a dream it's a dream.
    I understand how people see stuff.
        I could see stuff in nature—auras around things.

I was trying to go to sleep.
    Billy sat at the foot of my bed and he told me "I'm okay."
        But I couldn't deal with that until later.

Open casket, yellow turtleneck, his face and his expression
        twisted from the strangulation.
            Catholic funeral.
            One thing my brother's death did, my dad stopped drinking
And never came home drunk again.

My dad used to beat my brother all the time
    Throw him around the house
        Billy would cry, an animal-like cry, a moan

You never forget the sound of that moaning
    Those deep, deep cries.

He wasn't supposed to have a long hideous life on this planet.

Things happen for a reason.

tom

I think a lot of the abuse is born in the army.
    Either the Catholic church or the army.
        What kind of man was he?
I need to know what he came from.

Doreen gives him his food and he throws the food up to the ceiling
    Yelling and screaming
        Nightmares of plates flying

He'd drag us out of bed
    put us at the kitchen table, drunk, we're little kids
        listen to what I have to say I'm the head of the household

The abuse continued until I left but he did change.
    I think he was trying.
        I left, sixteen years old.

A year before that, Dad and Doreen had separated.
    Dad went by himself, kids went with Doreen.
        Much as I despised my stepmother, I was afraid to live
                             with my dad,

When I turned sixteen I met Lisa, my dear friend.
    I'd go to Lisa's house every weekend I could.
        I snuck back to Doreen's place to get my things.
Doreen slapped me and said "how can you do this to your father?"

This stuff destroys you forever
  but you get better at dealing with it.
    it's never going to go away.

I live in my mom's moan.
  They live in their mother's moan.
    My anger is about no justice for certain people.

Billy was kind, very close to me.
  This happened forty years ago and I still get a punch in the gut
    like it's the day after, because I hear the moan

It was a house of moans.

I wonder if my dad was drinking during those beatings.
  Throwing his food to the ceiling, white plates smashing in
the darkness.
    Ranting and raving about sluts and drunks.

Doreen sitting there letting him do it.

I called the police on my dad. I finally called the police.
  The police: "Oh, can you call back next week.
    Everyone is on deck for the G8 summit."

I had written my dad a letter.
    He wrote me back: "You kids turned out great."
      After I got that letter I called the cops.

A beautiful summer day.
    Penny's in the bedroom dying.
      "Call back later." Are you fucking kidding me?

If that man would've taken my call seriously that day
    my father might have been held accountable for his abuse.

I almost lost myself then.
    I had just found my mom, found her all messed up.
      My dad told me she had just left with some guy.
Who could blame her?
    She would go on to have another child after she left.
      Her name was Beverley.
      Beverley had a nice life, adopted out to the most wonderful
                     foster mother.
    She was the lucky one.

My mom has ten brothers and sisters
    but nobody knows where she is.

doreen

Doreen lost her hair during her terrible pregnancy
    with my stepsister. She wore a bad wig when she joined us.
        She was a single mother from Burton, New Brunswick
who answered an ad on a military bulletin board that Tom had posted
        (her own father was in the military)
            for a housekeeper / babysitter needed immediately.

She shows up with my little stepsister in her arms.
    "I'll take the job."
        Before we knew it, she was live-in.

Winter light, all of us kids, the house dusk, dark.
    We're all bundled up in winter coats sitting at an A&W
        Waiting for Doreen.

My stepsister was terrified of my dad
    but Doreen loved her and didn't love us.
        The abuse wasn't just sexual it was complete domination

Of everything. It just depended on what his mood was.
    Doreen couldn't do anything.
        It was never a loving partnership.

He put her down. He called her names.

She should never have looked after kids, her old base friends said.

She was a troubled person, would never thrive as a mother.

The minute she left my dad, she was with someone else.

to go back to 1969

New Brunswick.

    I don't remember my mother. The outline of a woman at the
top of the stairs.

        This was the last time she was near.

My first recollection of abuse was at 170 Saint John Avenue.

    Nightmares began during this time.

        The man next door, bearded, red hair.

He knew he could get me, somehow he knew I would not tell.

    I never did.

to go back to 1975

The family is posted to CFB Downsview.
    Doreen and my stepsister relocate too.
        We lived at Banks Court (Sheppard & Sunfield Ave.)
Dad was in Egypt/Cyprus for almost a year while we were here.

I was spending time with older kids, boys that were older.
    There was way too much sex stuff way too early.
        I'd already begun searching for love.

After Dad came home
    Billy was caught stealing from the local convenience store
        or was it a drugstore. My dad's army buddy's daughter
Worked as a clerk at that store and knew who Billy was.

Little did she know that telling about him stealing Ex-Lax
    and trying to return it for the lousy three bucks
        would bring him the beating of his life.

The beating was horrible. Unforgettable to this day.
Every little boy steals something, every little girl steals something,
    It's part of adolescence. I wonder if the clerk remembers squealing
        on my brother.

My son was caught stealing
    would be humiliation for my dad.

I loved school, loved my Grade Four teacher.

She took me to the Dairy Queen on my last day at Sheppard
Elementary.

I tried to tell her.

to go back to 1978

The family is posted to CFB Calgary in the spring of 1978,
    We move into a duplex on 20th St. S.W.
        Billy has been smoking again…grounded again, beaten again.

Dad makes Billy smoke an entire package of Colt cigars in one sitting.
    Making him sick to his stomach, humiliating him.

Billy has to sit on the floor at my father's feet in the living room
    with an ashtray and a pack of Colts. All the while my dad
        is sitting in his throne above him smoking cigarettes.

Billy is dead within days of this.
    My last conversation with my dear sweet Billy.
        Penny's last day of being a child.
Soon she would be taken while drunk and impregnated with her
                                                first child.

(to go to) october 2019

While I was working on her
    I ripped a hole in the foundation
        Two holes in her

I couldn't find her this time
    It took me twice as long, my confidence wasn't there
        Something in my universe wasn't right

It took all the pins, it didn't fit
    I had to put it all back on and do it right
        This time I wasn't going to get that fresh new piece

I wasn't
    I put her on my lap when I was working
        She wasn't looking at me this time

I didn't see her this time
    Hairs are falling out
        The moon is weird

I had been talking to Ian on the phone
    when the moan came out again about Billy being beaten
        by his father.

But there was no other reason for me to feel gloomy
    Other than the looming DNA results

The next day I got the test results.
No sign of McCrates or any other Irish people in my DNA.
The highest ranking member other than a maternal ancestor
Was a name i didn't recognize

A name I found pretty quickly in the census records I had looked
up a year ago!
He lived right next door to us. My dad must have been away
on exercise
When my mom and this guy got together.

I thought I would be overwhelmed with the McCrate connections
But no wonder there's no connection! They don't exist!
Which is wonderful. I don't have his blood in my veins

And my girls don't either!

Except for telling the whole world he was a shit
I don't need the McCrates anymore!
I don't need to worry about Aunt Elizabeth any more!

From what I've learned from the DNA Detectives website
(People looking for insight into their family stories)
Most of these people are adopted.

On DNA Detectives I'm stuck in the shock
The first person to answer me asked me
"Was this man you grew up with loving and caring?"

He was a monster.
So all the compassion pours in.
"I hope you find a nicer story."

I've had conversations with other members
But I haven't said *Search Angels, please help me*
I need to get to the bottom of this.

*("Search angels" are volunteers on a facebook group page where adoptees and
mothers who had to give away their babies go to find each other. Janet was
aware of three of these sites. There are hundreds of thousands of people on
these sites, she says. A lot of rejection, denial, and shame, but equally, a lot of
happy endings, she says.)*

If I can find a decent human being
if there's a wonderful aunt somewhere
I JUST WANT A STORY

What does "family of origin" mean when no one wants
to know who you are, or that you belong to them. Who
are you then? A motherless child and a fatherless child as
well? Tom was a monster, though he did try to be a dad at
times, she says. He told her that when he saw her for the
first time after she was born, all he could see was the scar
on her mouth from the surgery she had been given shortly
after birth. The child-mouth that he violated repeatedly for
years.

Trying to find her eldest brother, or links to Tom's
family, or people on her mother's side she might be able to
talk to or connect with, Janet did a DNA test with Ancestry
in September 2019. While waiting for the results, she
began to make a new wig, but it was proving difficult. Also,
she had spoken on the phone with her brother Ian, who
told her about his uncontrollable weeping, after years of
frozen feelings, for his brother Billy. "The moan" was alive
in the room.

valerie johnson

I don't hold it against my mom that she got pregnant
    My mom was twenty-five when she had me
        I was her fourth pregnancy

My mom had at least six children by five different men
    By the time she had me she was already messed up.
        She wasn't the kind of woman who could turn away

From someone coming on to her.
    She'd let them take her.
        She had some sexual trauma in her life.

Her first teenage pregnancy: maybe she was raped?

Was she taken advantage of? She was a weak Black woman of the
                                    sixties.
  A lot of women like her.
    What kind of strength or power could she have had?
She was probably called useless her whole life.

It was just a fantasy: from Diana Ross glamour to
    OMG you poor thing!
        To a three hundred and fifty pound vegetable to now a tramp.

Mental illness or not, she had choices!
She left us all, then had another baby, put her up for adoption
Left all these kids behind!

She was a fucking tramp
With no regard for the pain she left behind her!
Matthews probably had her doped up.

Do you realize who I am?
I'm your daughter.
Do you remember Tom?

She nods and she quietly says "yes." She knows who I am.
But she's so sick we're not going to be able to communicate.
So far gone there's nothing there for me.

Sitting here numb realizing the SOB wasn't my dad.
Robbed again. Everyone's fucking dead.
Cousins everywhere that I don't know.

I daydream about telling my mom off.
Real stories have to be told.
The earth is shaking with people wanting to know who
their family is.

I joined this Facebook free adoptee-search page.
    It's overwhelming reading the stories of rejection.
       Some beautiful stories but half are tragic:

"don't-ever-call-me-again-it's-not-your-business"
They're still kids
    and they need answers
       and they're never going to get them!

So overwhelmed, with the loss
    There's a lot of people who have no hope and it causes a
                              vicious circle of pain.
    It always comes back to that for me.

It's every human being's right to know who their biological father
is.

Your blood relatives saying "fuck off"
    Abuse is one thing
       A kick in the head is another thing

This rocks you to the core.
    I have so many "fuck you's" in my life.
       More than ever I'm discovering where I come from
And what family is supposed to mean.

I asked my grandfather's second wife about Cory, my mother's
first-born.
She didn't say to me, "that isn't true."
She said, "why can't you kids leave the past in the past?"

She hasn't contacted me since that day in 2003, just before Penny died.
She didn't get along with my mom.
You don't accept a stepmother.

ian

Look at how the children have suffered.
Penny, Billy, me. Beverley was given up for adoption.
Luckily for Ian he had a psyche that protected him.

Ian didn't take any beatings by my father after Billy died.
He'd gotten the fist but nothing like Billy.
Ian was good at staying out of trouble, just like me.

He didn't talk back. He did what he was told. No trouble at school.
He too was haunted by the moans of his brother being beaten
but his psyche was able to blank it out.

Ten years later all of a sudden he found himself
sobbing for his brother. He was way too young
barely ten years old and lost his big brother, his room-mate,
grounded for smoking a cigarette.
We were all addicted from my parents smoking in the house.
My dad gave me a carton of cigarettes for my fifteenth
birthday.
Probably symbolic to him.
As long as he could he kept up the sexual abuse.
Not until I left home did it stop.

There's a moan out there in the universe.
If you are quiet enough to listen
You hear a lot of things you don't usually hear.

Penny's living with me while she's dying.
　　In Calgary back in those days nurses would come to your home
　　　　and give you some respite, an hour to go away

And so I just happened to be chatting with the nurse one day
　　and she said, "well, with her Hepatitis C and everything…"
　　I just flipped and said "I've got kids in the house,

I need to know what's going on, I need her medical records."
　　So the doctors in Kingston gave me her entire file.

That booklet was two inches thick.
　　Cancer treatments, brought to Emergency by the police
　　　　Ambulance people finding her naked in the hallway

With a knife in her hand saying
　　"They're going to kill me!"
　　　　If it wasn't for the Hotel Dieu Catholic charity in Kingston

she would have died on the streets.

They paid for a social worker to hand her over to me.
　　Otherwise she would run away again.
　　　　When you get institutionalized
　　　　　　When your benefits run out
You go to a new town and set up a new file.
　　Kingston was the last stop on the railway that was her life.

the burning

After I lost Penny I couldn't handle it so I wrote a letter to my father
   Asking him to take responsibility. "You kids turned out great."
      I couldn't handle it. I lost all faith.

I was reading my own diaries.
   I needed to get this energy out of my world.
      What I didn't burn I threw in the garbage.

I believed that getting that stuff out of my house my office my
drawer
   Would get it out of my life.
      But it didn't.
         Everything just got worse.
      I thought this burning ritual would cleanse my mind.
But it didn't. Doreen had already lost everything.
   Every picture I've ever seen of myself as a child is gone.
      After I lost Penny I wanted to erase everything.
I had a bonfire in my backyard in Calgary right after Penny died.
   And into that bonfire I threw the envelope of Billy's hair.

Billy's funeral was open casket.
　　　It was something I should never have seen,
　　　　　his face in his casket. I'm standing there
　　　　　and I say to my dad, "I want some of his hair."
So my dad had the funeral guy cut some of his hair.

It was in a McGinnis & Holloway green envelope in my hope chest.
　　　I burned everything during that cleansing in the spring.
　　　　　I burned Billy's hair.

I wanted everything out of the house that signified those old dark days.
　　　I still feel guilty about not playing cards with him that day.
　　　　　I didn't throw his hair in the garbage, I burned it.
I was eleven years old when he died.

alopecia

The burning was in Calgary.
    That energy didn't stop for ten years.
      Kevin passed away in 2007.

For years after that I watched my youngest daughter falling apart
    She missed her father so badly.
      That's when my hair started falling out.

Just when I thought "I've made it, emotionally and professionally."
    Emotionally, past the pain; and professionally able to provide
                                    for my kids.
    But the universe said, *not so fast, you need to deal with this.*

I think I had to go bald to see myself, to lose my hair to start
looking
at myself, my physical health and emotional health.

I couldn't see the Gallant side of me until all my African curly hair
                                      fell out.
This whole journey is about recognizing myself.

I don't see Janet McCrate when I look in the mirror any more.
I haven't felt like a McCrate for decades.

It will be easier to take care of myself when my brain stops
                            spinning with all this shit.

Janet's hair, before it fell out, and when it began growing back as we worked on the text, was black. After she received the results of the DNA test, it fell out again. Today, it is growing back in platinum white, the legendary hair-turned-white-overnight of someone who has a bad shock.

kevin clift

Kevin and I met when I was nineteen and we married when I was
                                             twenty-two.
    I divorced Kevin in 1997 but we could never stay apart.
        I divorced him because he couldn't help me through this.

His career took him away from me and the kids for months at a time.
    I didn't want a husband who wasn't home.
        He was either away from us or laid off.

Kevin grew up in "Leave It to Beaver."
    He couldn't fathom what I had been through.
        But you realize nobody has a leave-it-to-beaver life.

We were living in Spring, Texas at the time.
    Kevin was a seismic surveyor in the oil industry.
        I hated Texas, I didn't want to go there and didn't like
                              being there.

My best friend while in Texas was Michael Bublé.
    We'd sing "Gotta Go Home" every time I got in my car.
I got to go home because on September 24, 2007
Kevin stepped out of his truck
and they he say he died before he hit the ground.

His father had died of the same condition.
They found his dad in a hotel room alone, away from his family,
at work. He was close to retirement.

The day Kevin died the kids and I were out on the patio.
                                                    The phone rang
        It was his sister-in-law Diane.
Kevin's unconscious, you've got to come & we'll go to the hospital together.
        The longest drive of my life, the girls in the back trying to
                                                    stay positive.
        Diane is hanging on to the steering wheel, holding back tears.

I think she knew already.
We get to the waiting area and all Kevin's work friends are there.
His friend Richard goes to hug me and Diane says, don't.
I think she wanted the nurse to tell me "I'm sorry he didn't make it."
The nurse told me and I fell to the ground and the kids fell on top of me.
Screaming my head off, I lost my shit.

It occurred to me I needed to see him
        So I walked down the hall
                It's like the soldier, the fireman, killed in the line of duty:
The first thing you see are their boots lined up nicely beside the bed.

Kevin was still there.

He was waiting for me.

But there was no way I'd let the kids see him.

I didn't want the kids' last vision of their father dead with a tube
in his mouth.

You want to kiss his lips to say goodbye and that horrible thing
was sticking out of his mouth.

Kevin was still there, though.

Two days later when I had to go see him at the funeral home
He was so long gone. Didn't even look like him.
They'd even changed his hair color.

Neither of my kids were criers but Samantha cried for days. She was
fifteen.

"Mom when am I going to stop crying."

We slept together, the three of us, for days.

I didn't want anything more to do with Texas.

I just wanted to go home, but I had to go home without Kevin.

I wasn't quite forty.

Kevin had been my best friend for more than half my life.

He was that confidante I needed for so long.

When he died, all of that died.

My in-laws let me down so bad.

They abandoned us.

They were not there for my kids.
    I realized no one was going to take care of me except myself.
       I remember exactly how I felt and saying it out loud.

I don't know how I got through those months.
I don't know how I got up and went to work.
My job was to be happy-go-lucky. Take care of everybody at the office.
How did I pull that off.

It wasn't until three years later my hair started falling out.
    We all have hair that falls on the bathroom floor
       There's always something in the shower drain

One day I scratched behind my ear and found a quarter-size bald spot
    I went to the doctor.
       "Looks like you have alopecia. I don't know what causes it."

He shot me up with cortisol twice
    "It may grow back or it may not."
       The internet said the same thing: autoimmune, stress.

Part of every day was my hair falling out.
    I'd sit in the sun and look down and hair would be all over
                            my blouse,
    I'd take my ponytail in my hand and hair would come out.

Within a year it was all gone.
 Ripping away at my confidence, like a lion's mane being cut off.
  Going from gorgeous curly hair that every hairdresser
Wanted to touch, to going to literally bald.
 You feel defeated.
  Three quarters of the way to going totally bald

I started wearing a wig.
 My first wig I bought from a lovely lady who ran a home business.
  A Jon Renot wig, it cost me $1500, one hundred percent
              human hair

But no cuticle left, no custom hairline, no glues, it just clipped on
 So the wind could literally blow my hair off.
I'm just now seeing myself losing my hair and becoming the wig-maker

The physical act of making wigs forced me to be by myself for hours
  and start laying out what went down
   I had to lose my hair and be at home making wigs
so that for the first time in my life
  I could see my universe clearly.

Tons of hair are exported every year to the West from poor countries. Some of it is sold to professional buyers; some of it is stolen or forcibly taken; some of it is donated. The demand in the West for temporary hair extensions, or "weaves," fuels much of this trade; full wigs are more costly owing to the price paid by middlemen for bundles of long, natural hair, and the labour involved in making a good-quality wig. "Temple hair," the only hair Janet will use for her wigs, is obtained from young women undergoing puberty rituals in India. At the temples in India, barbers shave the young woman's head of waist-length hair, which has been offered as a sacrifice, and sell it to buyers willing and eager to purchase it. Janet is aware of the ethical issues the human hair industry involves and ensures that the hair she buys is from certified dealers. A complete wig requires Janet to ventilate about 80,000 individual hairs. Every wig she makes is an individual. Wigs, as we all know, are powerful transformational magic.

cold calling

There's a seam I want to weave in
    a page called Cold Calling
        always putting myself out there
I hate it when you have to do it for yourself instead of for a
                              company product.
    I have Cold Calling notes on my phone
        hello Auntie Mae
        hello Dobbin
        hello Gallants
All this rejection. How terrifying it can be. G— and H—
    don't understand it's not about vengeance
        it's about a peaceful coming to this family.

It amazes me now that I realize what happened to my mom
    and her siblings. She never had a mom that nurtured her.
        Penny had the same gene missing.
Somehow I was spared.

When I say that it's such a success for me
    to have nurtured two beautiful girls who are healthy

    and feel loved
and will know how to nurture their children—
    That's the happy ending!

But I'm still looking for my mom
	and looking for my mom's husband
		I'm focusing on the Windsor obits

I've left word at two possible nursing homes, one right in Windsor
	where you go when you're a social services client
		but unless I'm the Executor I can't have access

they will leave my name and number
	and it's up to that person to call
		but no one has called.

Cold calling, it's hard, scary, setting yourself up for more rejection.
	You have to be this saleswoman.
		It's the strangest place to be in.

Janet was able to locate one of the four children of Reg
Gallant, who arranged for Janet to meet him and his three
brothers and sisters. Ray Gallant was the Gallant living
downstairs from the McCrates and who is most likely
Janet's biological father. Ray Gallant—whose obituary
photograph shows a strong resemblance to Janet—died
four months before Janet had the results of the DNA test.
Ray's brother Reg, however, whom Janet also resembles,
also lived and worked in the same city, so there was
a chance that he, rather than Ray, may have fathered
Janet; in which case these four children of Reg Gallant
would be Janet's half-siblings. However, much to Janet's
disappointment, another DNA test revealed that Reg's
children are Janet's cousins, not her half-siblings; and that
G—who still refuses to acknowledge Janet's paternity—is
her half-sibling. She says she would welcome a relationship
with him and his family if only for two reasons: to have
and hold pictures of her father's face, and to have a
narrative of his character.

and now i'm found

I just need to breathe through this chapter.

I am over-filled with joy
    but I'm overwhelmed.

Steven and the cousins are saying
    "we had a wonderful time, too,
        everyone's talking about how much they enjoyed
                meeting you."

Cousin Lisa, who's really funny, said Ray was a "horn dog, all
                three of them were."
    The ones still living are old, all ears and nose,
        the resemblance is so in my face
          and it's been peeking at me for months:

REG, IS THAT YOU? RAY, IS THAT YOU?

Now that I'm allowed to see it
    I see it
        and embrace it. I don't need G— to do a DNA test.

Just like going to Auntie Mae's house
    and seeing Penny's expression on her face
        I know I'm related.
        Auntie Mae said, "you're just like your mother."
My mother was very beautiful and kind.

I feel like I'm home, finally.
    It's so powerful.
        I haven't been this excited about the future.

I have awesome cousins.
    I no longer need my Gallant half-sibling's permission
        To be me,
            Janet Gallant

afterword
Sharon Thesen

"Women's stories are different," writes Svetlana Alexievich, "and about different things." What strikes me about the way Janet tells her story is how much of it is about her love for and care of her siblings, her attempts to understand her mother's and her father's behaviour, her desire to know more about their family histories, to have a relative tell her something, anything, an anecdote, a memory, a rumour. So she could put together an explanation. "I just want a story," she says. But no one wants to talk to her. *Leave the past in the past,* they say.

But it turns out that this telling, the text of *The Wig-Maker,* is the story that has begun to show her her true identity. "The universe was telling me this all along," she says.

During the two and a half year course of our conversations, Janet was researching obituary notices and social media links and census records. Who lived next door to whom. Who had musical talent; who as an Irish-descended boy had gone to a Catholic church in the 1940's and 50's in Nova Scotia; who her pregnant and unemployed mother had worked for as a housekeeper prior to moving in with her father. And what happened to her mother's first child, born to her as a teenager in the small Black community of Wildwood, Alberta? Janet longs to know her eldest half-brother. Who is the father of her half-sister Penny? She has a pretty good idea. How many other children did Janet's mother give birth to after she left the McCrate family? Janet knows of one girl who was adopted out as a baby, "the lucky one—she had a good life." And what in her father's life resulted in his having been "such a monster"?

And then, looking for possible relatives she could contact, Janet does a DNA test through Ancestry.com, only to find out that she was not related at all to Tom McCrate. "Gallant" was the surname on her paternal side. According to census records, a man named Gallant lived in the same two-storey house in Calgary as the McCrate family, in the first floor suite, at the time Janet was conceived in June 1966 while her father likely was away on military exercise. When she came over to show me the DNA test results, I didn't know what I was looking at, until Janet pointed out there was not a single McCrate listed, only Gallants. It took a while for this to sink in. "You mean, Tom McCrate is not your father?" I asked.

II

In her introduction to the oral histories she recorded in *The Unwomanly Face of War*, about Soviet women fighters in World War II, Svetlana Alexievich writes, "each of these stories is composed of many persons: the one who is talking now, in the present; the one who all this happened to, in the past; and her, the listener, the recorder." For this story, I would add the person whose wig-making and remembering and researching was revealing not only her genetic identity, but the spiritual energies of her life as both victim and survivor. Only in retrospect did we come to realize that the process of telling this history while she was also constructing the different "selves" each new wig came to be, was answered by the DNA test results. But having the DNA test results was again just the beginning of a new search for answers that proved even more frustrating and hurtful. Janet researched her new paternal name and found a photograph of a man whom Janet strongly resembles, whom she was able to contact, and who had died just months previous to Janet receiving her DNA test results. This man's family, except for a cousin Janet was matched with and whom she able to contact, did not trust Janet's story or the validity of her claims to kinship. They wanted nothing to do with her, she says.

Janet and I met when she and her partner Jim moved in across the street in 2017. She told me on a couple of occasions that she had a story to tell. She wouldn't hear of trying to write it herself so I said I'd write down what she said and give it back to her, to get her going on her story. At the time I had no idea what was in store. She would come over, we'd sit together in my study, and I typed what I could of what she was saying. We had more and more meetings. My doing the physical writing spared Janet the anxieties and uncertainties of composition. It also allowed for space and freedom and emotion and trust. These were not sound recordings, nor was I "taking dictation"—so there were and are gaps. My listening was somehow transferred to the computer screen without my having time to organize it in any way. I wrote the lines and sentences as she was talking but I also included spaces and silences—the original transcripts are fragmentary. At times I worried whether I was qualified to respond to Janet's words in a therapeutically correct way—but the well-meanings of therapy were not the reason for these revelations. The reason was the sound of the story we'd somehow decided to make together—"the moan"—the moan of a soul, the moan of her feelings, her brother Billy's moan, and at times my own quiet moaning while my hands were moving over the keyboard.

But for a long time I had no idea how we were going to proceed, since by then (several months into the project) we had decided we wanted to make this story into a book manuscript. I could not, would not, try to write it in third person. Janet's telling was going to compose the entirety of the text—her telling processed through my ears, my heart, my hands. The text became a long poem in Janet's voice, lineated in triadic stepped-line stanzas—loosely speaking. Triads seemed to lend themselves most readily to the rhythms of her voice and also to the overall tone of the story. (Tercets and triads often occur in poetic narration of epic, tragic, or elegiac content.) Even so, the bulk of Janet's narration remains in the rough transcripts. Some of the episodes of abuse have been omitted from this account. Details of their father's sexual abuse of her sister Penny are known to Janet but not to me. "We talked about everything, and I mean everything," Janet says, about the time she was caring for Penny in the last months of her life. "Poor Penny didn't get over it," she says, "but I survived, even though you never get over it." Generations of pain never get settled. "I find myself in moments of rejection back in the same horrible place," Janet says. " It's just like grieving. I can be strong, I can move on. But, much as you try…"

Janet's initial attempts to make contact with her newly-discovered paternal relatives met with resistance, anger, silence, rejection. She had no doubt one of the reasons for this was that the extramarital affair was conducted with a Black woman. She talked about the dismal feeling of making cold call after cold call

to possible half-siblings, cousins, aunts or uncles, in addition to
the earlier disappointing searches for people who might be able
to supply information as to the whereabouts of her mother, or the
whereabouts of her eldest brother.

Janet's mother, Valerie Johnson, was born in the small Black
community of Wildwood, Alberta. Janet's second cousin, Deborah
Dobbins, made a film called *We Are the Roots*, which describes
the establishment of several Black communities in Alberta and
Saskatchewan in the early 1900's. The Canadian government had
put out a call for people to homestead in northern Alberta and
Saskatchewan. They would be given 160 acres for a $10 fee. The
$10 fee and the agreement that forty percent of the land parcel had
to be seeded and cropped was, as Dobbins says, "a minor price to
pay" for freedom from segregation and second-class citizenship
in Oklahoma, where most of these settlers came from after Jim
Crow laws had been instituted in that State. There was trouble at
the border, however; Blacks were not really all that welcome in
Alberta, and by 1911 the government of Wilfred Laurier prohibited
further migration, citing "unsuitability for the climate of Canada."
But as Dobbins says, "we came anyway. We had the money, we had
the skills, we had everything on the checklist." They crossed rivers
and creeks and bug-infested muskeg and built houses, a school,
a church. They were harassed by the Edmonton branch of the Ku
Klux Klan, which was blatantly active on the Prairies in the 1930's.
There are stories of burning crosses, Klansmen on horseback.

One person who was born into this story, whose parents had
lost whatever roots and community they had in Oklahoma where
they were free to own property and where they inter-married with

indigenous people, was Valerie Johnson, Janet's mother, whose own mother was an adopted-out descendent of Little Dove and Harvey Converse, a plantation owner. Valerie's grandfather, Frank Johnson, was one of Wildwood's most distinguished pioneers. Born in Dallas, Texas, he had been reluctant to leave Oklahoma, but in the end he became an iconic centenarian citizen of Wildwood (formerly Junkins), Alberta, famous for his style, his cane, his hat. His portrait, enlarged to several storeys in height, was one of the posters adorning the opening of the new Royal Museum of Alberta in Edmonton in 2018. An exhibit inside the museum was devoted to the Black communities of Wildwood and Amber Valley. The restaurant sign advertising Janet's great-aunt Mae's pies was exhibited there, as was Frank Johnson's hat and cane.

After the desertion of her own birth mother, Janet's mother Valerie Johnson was raised by her father's second wife, who went on to have eleven more children. Janet sees her mother as a young girl in Wildwood already suffering from a diagnosed mental illness and in the hostile care of a stepmother and eleven half-siblings. Nobody seems to know what happened to the baby that teenage Valerie gave birth to in Wildwood, except that he probably was adopted by a family in Edmonton. By the time Janet was born in 1967, Valerie had given birth to a son given up for adoption, to Penny (father unknown), and to Billy with Janet's father. Her younger brother Ian followed Janet by 14 months. Valerie deserted the family in 1970, never to have contact with any of them again. Since Janet had not seen or heard from her mother for the next thirty years, she wonders if she has half-siblings she doesn't know about. This curiosity was part of Janet's motivation to undergo DNA testing.

The question of who you are and who you belong to could never be completely answered by a DNA test. Something forensic, but ultimately mysterious and unhelpful, disturbing and chaotic, is revealed by these lists of unknown relatives and dippers into the genetic pool of one's former invisible past. Something of this energy was present, and revealed, the day that Janet, in her wig-making studio, with the block-head held in her lap while her fingers fumbled with the pins, and a windstorm tossed the spruce branches outside her window, the day before the results arrived with the news that her father wasn't really her father after all. Even so, he was the only father she ever knew. And she never knew her mother, even though she really was, or is, her actual mother.

I am eager, as the conduit of this tale, to try to propose the nature of its mystery. I found a sense of its workings in *Race and the Cosmos* by Rev. Dr. Barbara A. Holmes. She says that it is "idolatrous" to believe that "any manifestation of personhood can be defined by one idea or another."

> "We can say that the quantum world exists, but its contours are elusive and potential rather than actual...The possibility of mutuality still beckons us, because no person or society can fill the categories...permanently and totally. We are creatures of potential and possibility, embodying many aspects of reality simultaneously."

Working on her block-heads, Janet is encountering a "strange intelligence," that "germ of the future which is being formed within us in mysterious connection with the outer world, and knows what will happen to us in the future," writes Victoria Nelson in *The Secret Life of Puppets*. She writes that "the doll or mannequin comes to life through the efforts of a charismatic creator or soul-bestower" and that "far from being a mechanical operation, manipulation of the puppet would require total identification of operator and puppet: the operator [herself] would have to dance." Nelson includes tailors' dummies in the same imaginarium as "puppet-idols poised at the brink of a new adventure in the world." This co-operation of "puppet" and "operator" (or wig and wig-maker) supports the uncanny sensation of emerging personhood at a certain point of the wig-making process, and the dynamic relationship between maker and made. The mystery of this dynamism I feel was also present in Janet's and my meetings; we too were unknowingly co-creating a "new adventure in the world."

Who is the teller in this story, and who is the listener, and who is the recorder? As Alexievich writes, "I often see how they sit and listen to themselves. To the sound of their own soul. They check it against the words." You do this, she says, to "to answer your own question: Why did all this happen to me? You gaze at everything, almost from the other side. [There is] no longer any need to deceive anyone or yourself." I want to say here that I am immensely grateful to poets John Lent and Jake Kennedy for their recommendation to me of Alexievich's book. Her book records the harrowing memories of Soviet women who fought in World War II and survived; but in Alexievich's non-intrusive approach, I felt a smidgeon of kinship, and a huge appreciation for what she says about these women and their ways of talking about their experiences—not to mention how devastating their experiences were, even to read about.

"I listen," Alexievich says. And she says, "Pain is the proof of past life. There are no other proofs. I don't trust other proofs. Words have more than once led us away from the truth. I think of suffering as the highest form of information, having a direct connection with mystery. With the mystery of life." When asked by a friend of hers why she was "doing this," Janet told her that she wanted the world to say her brother's and her sister's names just once; to know what they went through. And that she wants someone to grieve for Penny, even if just for a moment.

acknowledgements

Paul Mier

Jim Pinter

Jenny Penberthy

Nancy Wood

Rolf Maurer

William Carlos Williams

Diane di Prima

Ed Sanders

Victoria Nelson

Jodey Castricano

John Lent

Jake Kennedy

Rev. Dr. Barbara A. Holmes

Svetlana Alexievich

Grant Point

Lisa Kawalauskis

Robert Gallant

Steven Gallant

Lisa Smith

CD Wright